THE SILLY SKYSCRAPER

GENESIS 11:1-9 FOR CHILDREN

Written by Virginia Mueller

Illustrated by Vaccaro Associates/Catherine Leary

ARCH Books

Copyright © 1970 BY CONCORDIA PUBLISHING HOUSE,
ST. LOUIS, MISSOURI

MANUFACTURED IN THE UNITED STATES OF AMERICA
ISBN 0-570-06050-8

D0324778

Old Noah's descendants
were gathered one day
to settle the question
of where they should stay.

They asked one another,
"Why should we divide
and travel to settle
this earth far and wide?

"We'll stay here together,
for this is our home.
We don't want to travel.
We don't want to roam."

They built a great city,
the best one around.
A bigger or better one
could not be found.

"We are best," bragged the people.
King Nimrod agreed.
He said, "There's another
great thing that we need.

"Our city of Babel
is greatest, it's true;
but now we must build
a tall tower here too.

"This monument here
on the plain of Shinar
will make us a name
that is known near and far."

The king made a list
of the things they would need
and from his big army
chose ten men to lead.

Then workmen were chosen.
Each one had a task.
There wasn't a person
that they didn't ask.

Some men drew the plan,
and some chose the site.
They checked and rechecked,
for this had to be right.

The women chopped straw
to be mixed with the clay.
They molded and fired
the bricks day by day.

The oxen were used
to pull timbers and boulders,
and baskets of mortar
were carried on shoulders.

Some tended the vineyards.
Some harvested wheat
and other good food
that was needed to eat.

The children helped also
by gathering sticks
to use in the kilns
where they fired the bricks.

They tended the babies,
small sisters and brothers
while tending the sheep
was the task of still others.

No task was too great.
No task was too small.
King Nimrod declared,
"There is work here for all.

"This tower must reach
above clouds in the sky.
Work harder and faster!
We must build it high!"

"We'll be greater than God,"
one man called from the top.
"We must reach the heavens
before we can stop."

Now God was displeased
when He saw their tall tower.
With only one language
they had too much power.

So God chose a way
of His own, new and wise.
One day all the builders
had quite a surprise.

Their words were mixed up,
and they all sounded silly.
No one understood,
and they ran willy-nilly.

A foreman called out
for more bricks, and instead
they brought him a turban
to cover his head.

Instead of some water
the women brought straw,
instead of a shovel
a sharp, cutting saw.

When someone called, "Up,"
instead they went down.
Soon all of the workmen
were wearing a frown.

The people were angry
and started to fight.
With all the new languages
nothing went right.

They put down their tools,
and they left one by one.
All work stopped completely.
No more could be done.

The people of Babel
began to divide.
Those with the same language
lined up side by side.

Some groups traveled eastward.
Some moved to the west.
While other groups thought
north or south would be best.

The silly skyscraper
was left there alone
to crumble and fall
into pieces of stone.

DEAR PARENTS:

This is a story of pride and judgment.

The people decided to build a tall tower as a way of making a name for themselves. They were proud people determined to build a monument to their own glory. The unity of their common language and their building skills were not used for God, because they forgot that all things came from the creative and loving power of God.

The Lord saw their silly skyscraper and the pride of their hearts. He brought them to judgment by confusing their language. They stopped their tower building and scattered everywhere.

The story in this Archbook ends with the judgment of God on proud people, but the story of the Bible continues with the hope and mercy God gave to Abraham. God had mercy and forgave all who believed His word of agreement. His gracious agreement was completed and fulfilled in the coming of Jesus Christ.

You will find this story useful to help your child recognize "silly skyscrapers" today, for any actions done out of pride instead of love for God stand under His judgment. But do not stop there. Go on to teach your child that Jesus Christ has come to forgive our pride and to make us His servants who live and build for the Lord.

THE EDITOR